Number and Operations

Nature's Delicate Balance

Contents

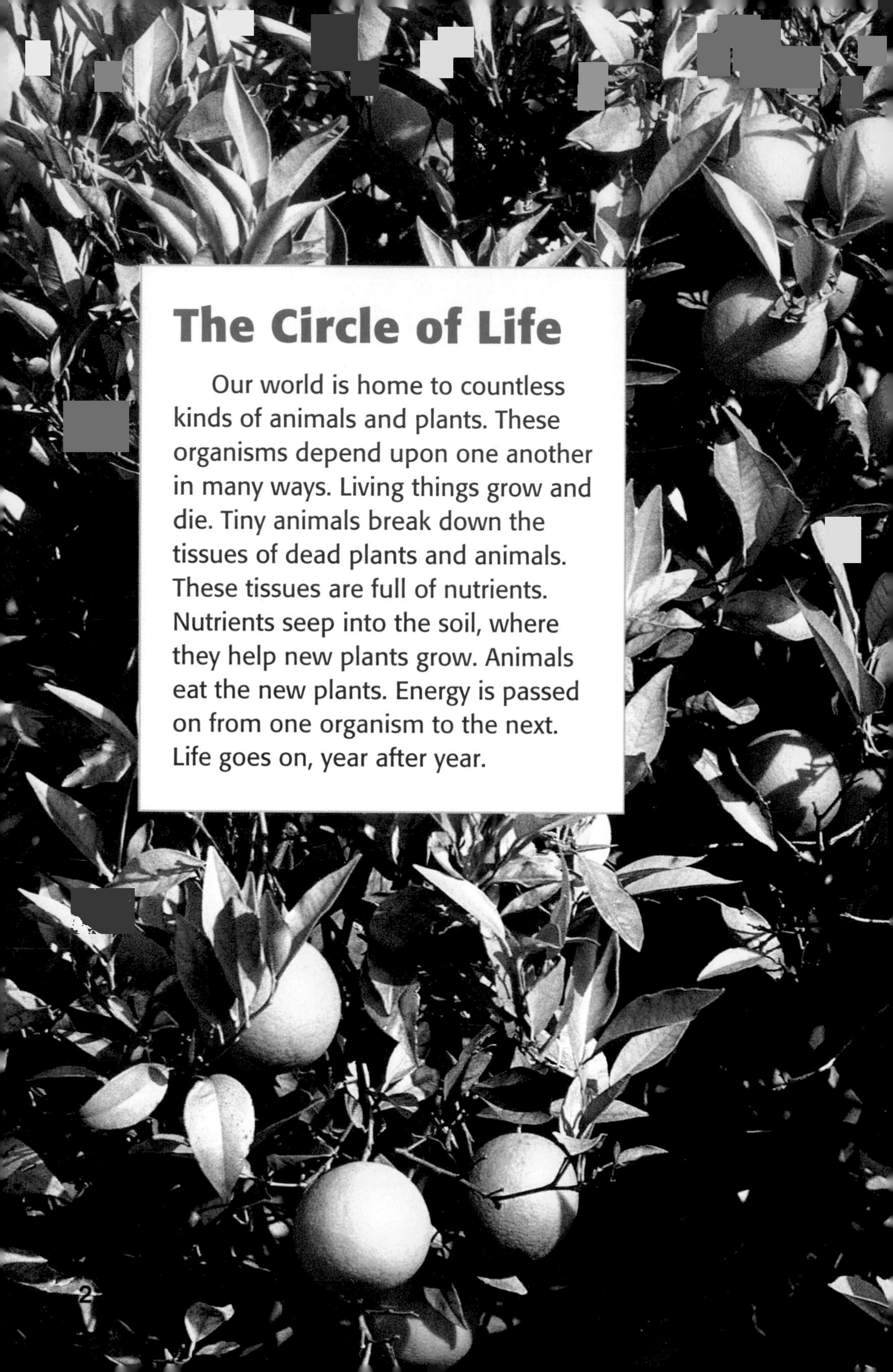

The Circle of Life

Our world is home to countless kinds of animals and plants. These organisms depend upon one another in many ways. Living things grow and die. Tiny animals break down the tissues of dead plants and animals. These tissues are full of nutrients. Nutrients seep into the soil, where they help new plants grow. Animals eat the new plants. Energy is passed on from one organism to the next. Life goes on, year after year.

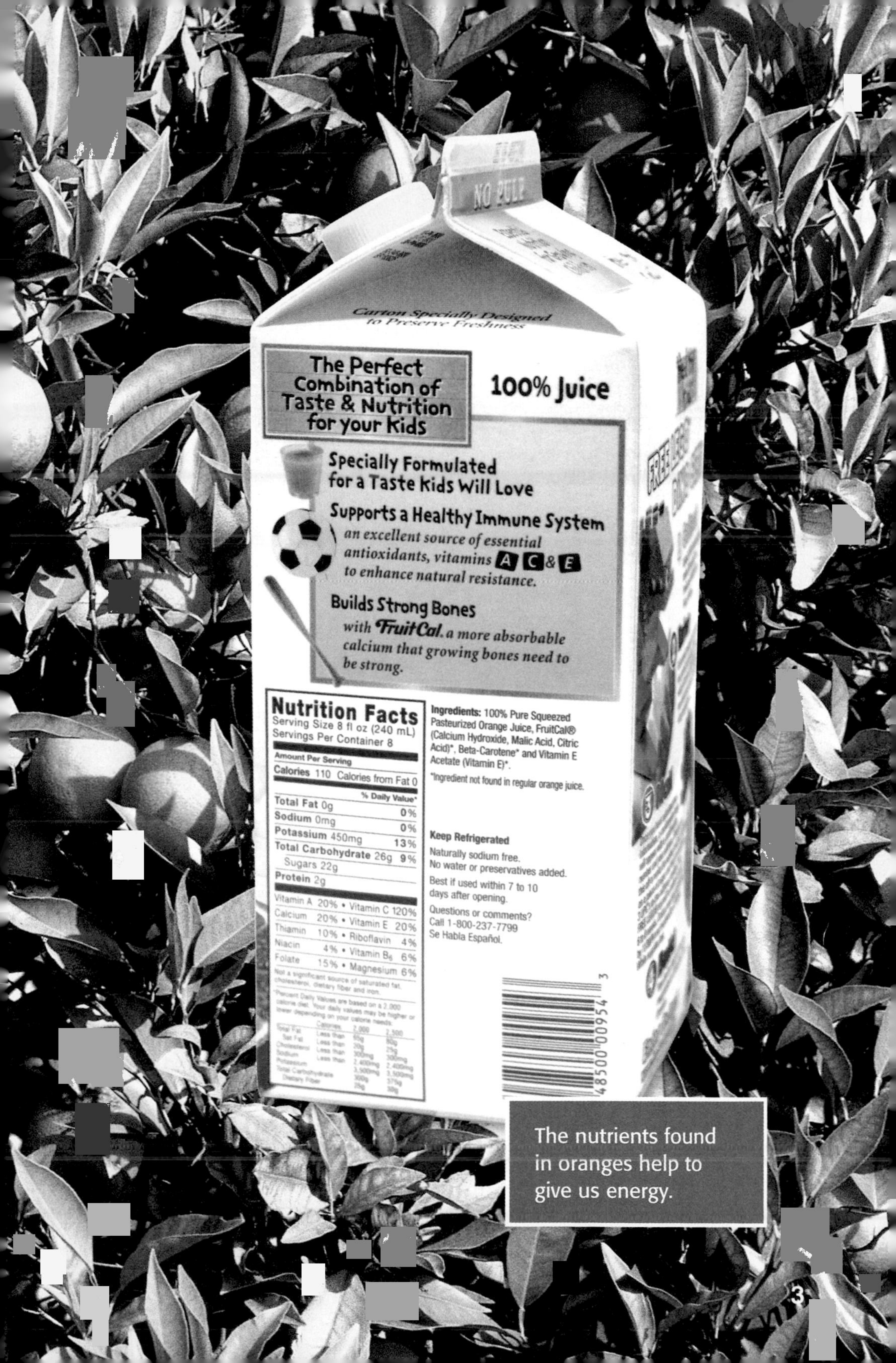
NO PULP
Carton Specially Designed to Preserve Freshness
The Perfect Combination of Taste & Nutrition for your Kids
100% Juice
Specially Formulated for a Taste Kids Will Love
Supports a Healthy Immune System
an excellent source of essential antioxidants, vitamins A C & E to enhance natural resistance.
Builds Strong Bones
with FruitCal, a more absorbable calcium that growing bones need to be strong.
Nutrition Facts
Serving Size 8 fl oz (240 mL)
Servings Per Container 8
Amount Per Serving
Calories 110 Calories from Fat 0
% Daily Value*
Total Fat 0g 0%
Sodium 0mg 0%
Potassium 450mg 13%
Total Carbohydrate 26g 9%
Sugars 22g
Protein 2g
Vitamin A 20% • Vitamin C 120%
Calcium 20% • Vitamin E 20%
Thiamin 10% • Riboflavin 4%
Niacin 4% • Vitamin B6 6%
Folate 15% • Magnesium 6%
Ingredients: 100% Pure Squeezed Pasteurized Orange Juice, FruitCal® (Calcium Hydroxide, Malic Acid, Citric Acid)*, Beta-Carotene* and Vitamin E Acetate (Vitamin E)*.
*Ingredient not found in regular orange juice.
Keep Refrigerated
Naturally sodium free.
No water or preservatives added.
Best if used within 7 to 10 days after opening.
Questions or comments?
Call 1-800-237-7799
Se Habla Español.

The nutrients found in oranges help to give us energy.

All life on Earth's surface depends on the Sun. The Sun provides Earth with energy in the form of sunlight. The energy in sunlight is taken in by plants. Plants are called producers because they use energy from the sun to produce, or make, their own food. Plants store this food in their tissues. They use some of the food as they live and grow. The rest stays stored inside the plant's tissues.

When animals eat plants, they consume, or take in, the energy stored in plants. Animals are called consumers because they consume energy. Animals cannot make their own food. They must eat other living things to get the energy they need to live and grow.

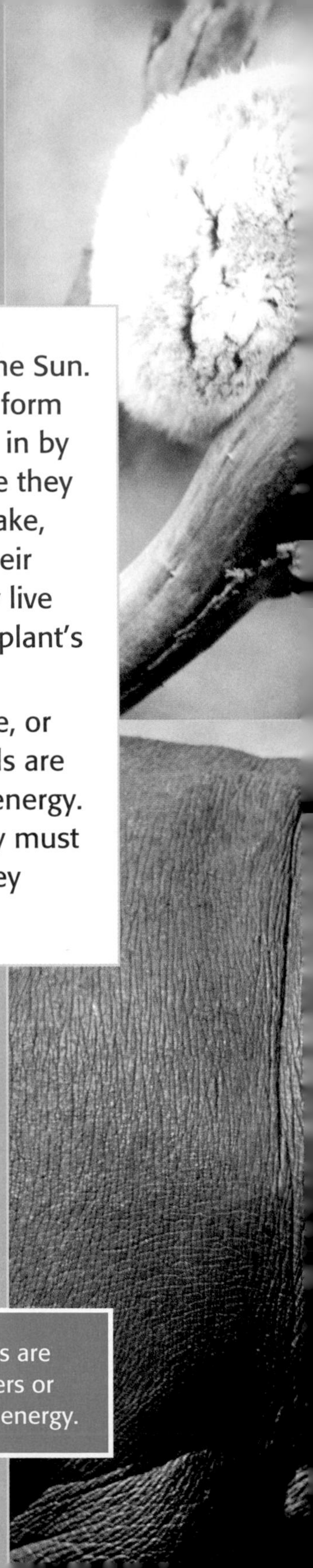

All living things are either producers or consumers of energy.

Koalas eat 200 to 500 grams of eucalyptus leaves per day.

Herbivores, Carnivores, and Omnivores

Different kinds of animals eat different foods. Some animals eat only plants and things that come from plants. Animals that eat only plant foods are called **herbivores**. Elephants, giraffes, koalas, cows, sheep, horses, deer, rabbits, guinea pigs, and many kinds of birds are herbivores.

Herbivores eat whole plants and plant parts, such as leaves, roots, and stems. They eat food that plants make, such as fruits, berries, nuts and seeds. Their bodies are designed to digest plant foods. Plants have all the nutrients herbivores need to eat.

Did You Know?

Giraffes can spend from 16 to 20 hours per day eating.

Some kinds of animals eat only the bodies of other animals. Animals that eat other animals are called **carnivores**. Foxes, lions, sharks, and birds of prey are carnivores. They will eat the meat and eggs of other animals. Most carnivores will hunt and kill animals, then eat them.

Carnivores know by instinct which animals they can and cannot eat. For example, a bat will hunt for insects at night to eat. However, a bat will not try to grab a horse or a cow. The bat only hunts animals that it is able to kill and eat.

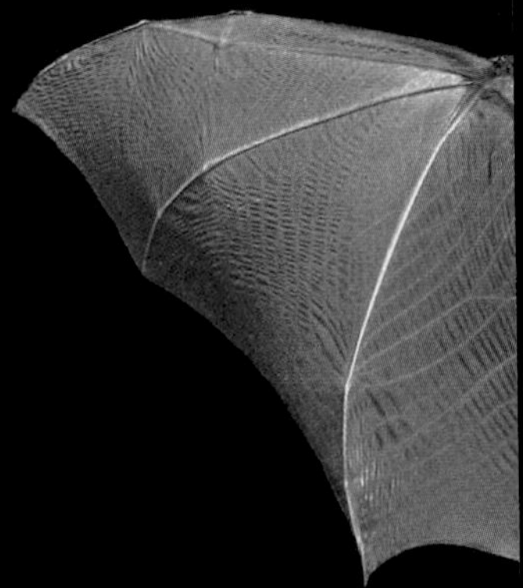

Did You Know?

One reason hawks are such good hunters is eyesight. A hawk can see eight times better than a human can.

Some bats eat up to
2,000 insects in one night.

Some animals are able to eat and digest all kinds of foods. Animals that eat plants and other animals are called **omnivores**. These animals will eat leaves, roots, fruit, nuts, seeds, insects, fish, snakes, worms, and other animals. If they are hungry enough, omnivores will eat almost anything! Raccoons, skunks, opossums, wild pigs, grizzly bears, black bears, crows, seagulls, blue jays, and even some kinds of mice are omnivores.

Did You Know?

Many humans eat both plants and animal products. This makes humans omnivores.

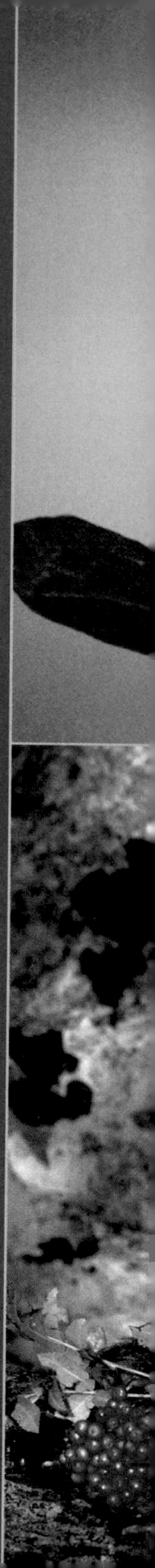

Omnivores eat different kinds of foods, including plants and other animals.

Special Body Structures

Herbivores, carnivores, and omnivores all have certain body structures that help them survive. Some animals have horns or tusks that help them fight and defend themselves. Some animals have strong legs that allow them to run away from danger.

One of the most important body structures animals have is their teeth. Herbivores have large back teeth that are made for grinding plant fibers. Carnivores have sharp pointed teeth that are made for biting and tearing meat. Omnivores have teeth that are made for eating all kinds of foods.

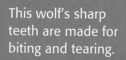

This wolf's sharp teeth are made for biting and tearing.

The World's Fastest Land Animals	
Animal	**Speed (miles per hour)**
Cheetah	70
Pronghorn antelope	61
Lion	50
Quarter horse	48
Elk	45

All animals must eat in order to survive. It may seem cruel that some animals kill other living creatures, but it is a natural part of life. Every creature has the body structures to get what it needs from its environment. Our world has a balanced system of life and death.

A snake can eat something that is three times larger than its own mouth.

TALK ABOUT IT

Why do you think it is important that different types of animals eat different foods? What might happen if all animals ate the same thing?

This Venn diagram shows an example of the foods eaten by herbivores, carnivores, and omnivores. Look at the diagram and notice how balanced the three parts are. Note that while omnivores eat foods from both circles, herbivores and carnivores eat different things.

What Animals Eat

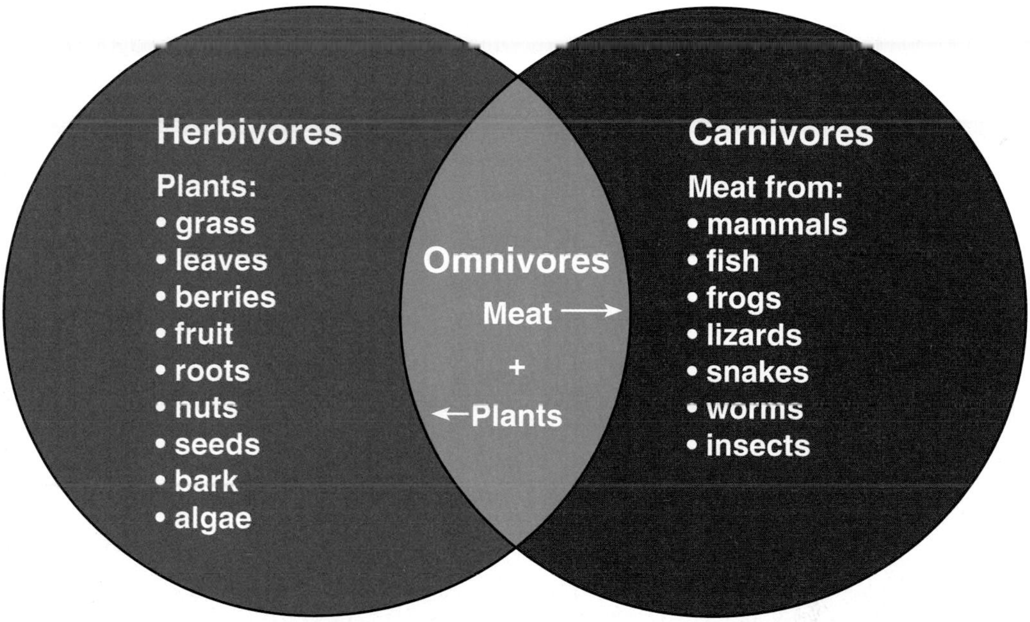

Food Chains

Each plant and animal plays an important role in the circle of life. Some living things provide what other living things need. Plants make the oxygen in the air that animals breathe. Plants are nutritious food for animals. Animals release a gas called carbon dioxide into the air when they breathe out. Plants need carbon dioxide to grow. Animals also add nutrients back to the soil through waste. These nutrients help plants grow.

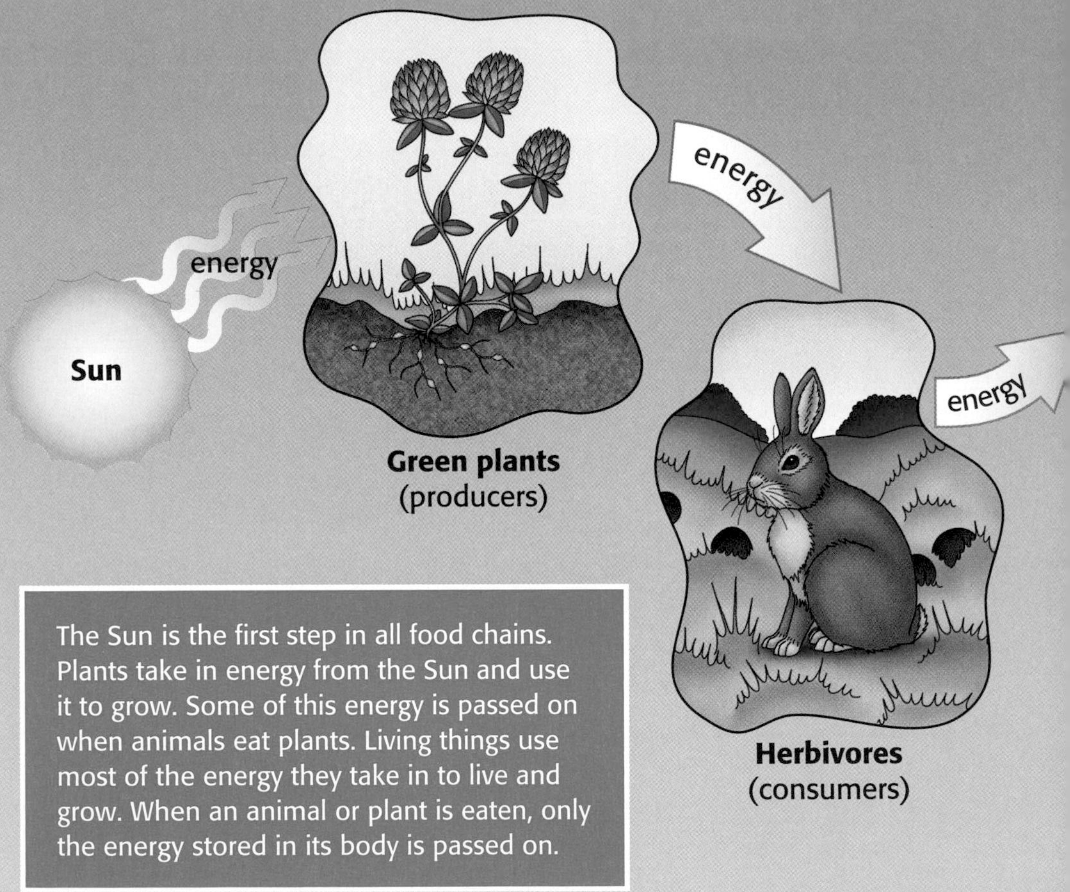

The Sun is the first step in all food chains. Plants take in energy from the Sun and use it to grow. Some of this energy is passed on when animals eat plants. Living things use most of the energy they take in to live and grow. When an animal or plant is eaten, only the energy stored in its body is passed on.

Both plants and animals are important to the health of every living thing on Earth. You can think of each living organism on Earth as a link in a chain. The diagram below shows how each living thing gets what it needs from other living things.

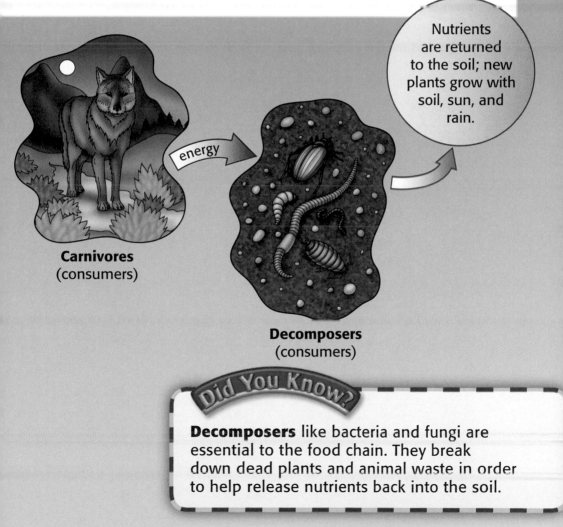

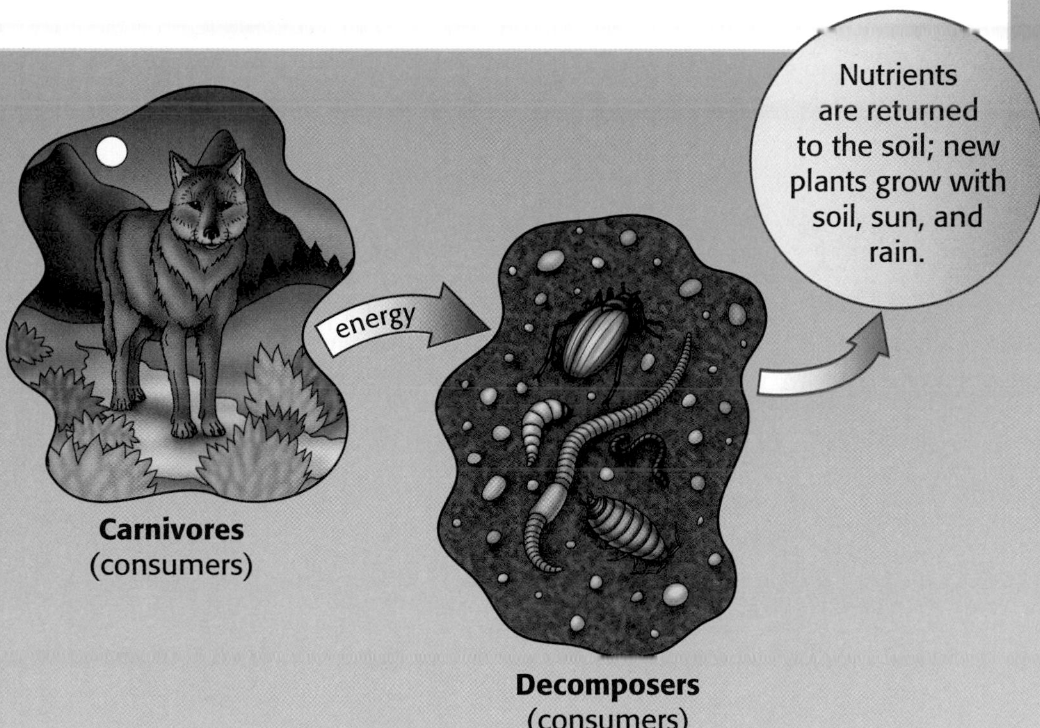
Nutrients are returned to the soil; new plants grow with soil, sun, and rain.
energy
Carnivores
(consumers)
Decomposers
(consumers)

Did You Know?

Decomposers like bacteria and fungi are essential to the food chain. They break down dead plants and animal waste in order to help release nutrients back into the soil.

Healthy Ecosystems

When ecosystems are healthy, every living thing has what it needs. When ecosystems are unhealthy because there are too many of some kinds of animals and too few of others, animals will go hungry and die.

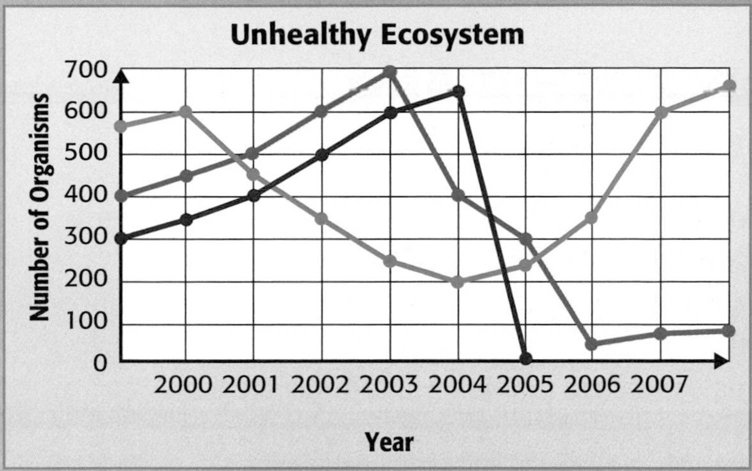

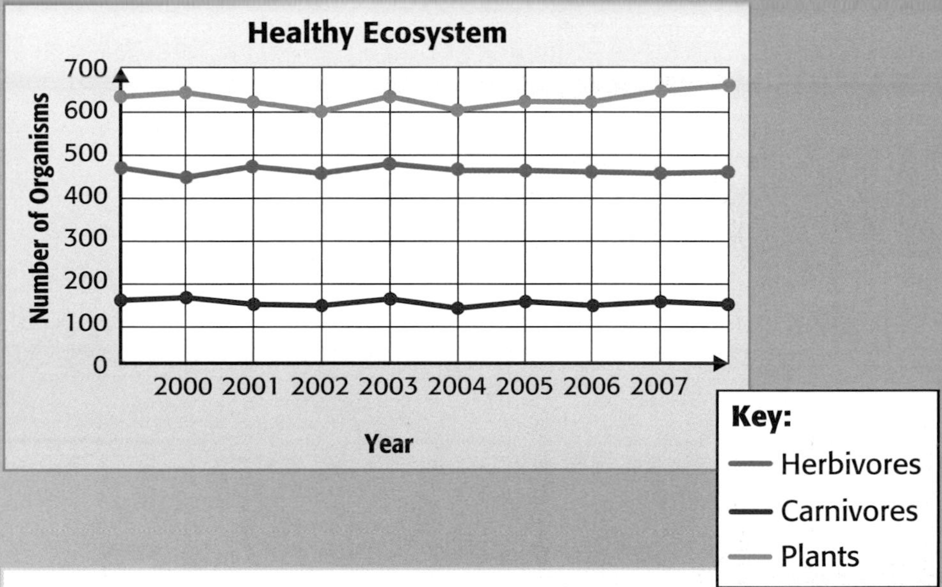

Notice that when the number of herbivores goes up, the number of plants goes down but the number of carnivores goes up. When the plants are gone, herbivores have nothing to eat, so they will die off. When there are no more herbivores, the carnivores have nothing to eat and they die off. In healthy ecosystems, there is a balance of consumers and producers. Populations do not get too large or too small. Every animal has enough to eat.

Deforestation and Reforestation

You now know that it is important for our ecosystems to have the right numbers of plants, herbivores, and carnivores. However, many times nature is out of balance. Natural and human-made changes that happen to ecosystems can cause plants and animals to die.

Deforestation can be one reason that nature is out of balance. Deforestation happens when large amounts of forests are cleared. Drought, fires, slash-and-burn farming techniques, and urban development are all forms of deforestation. The result is that animals who live there will often die.

United States Old-Growth Forests Over Time

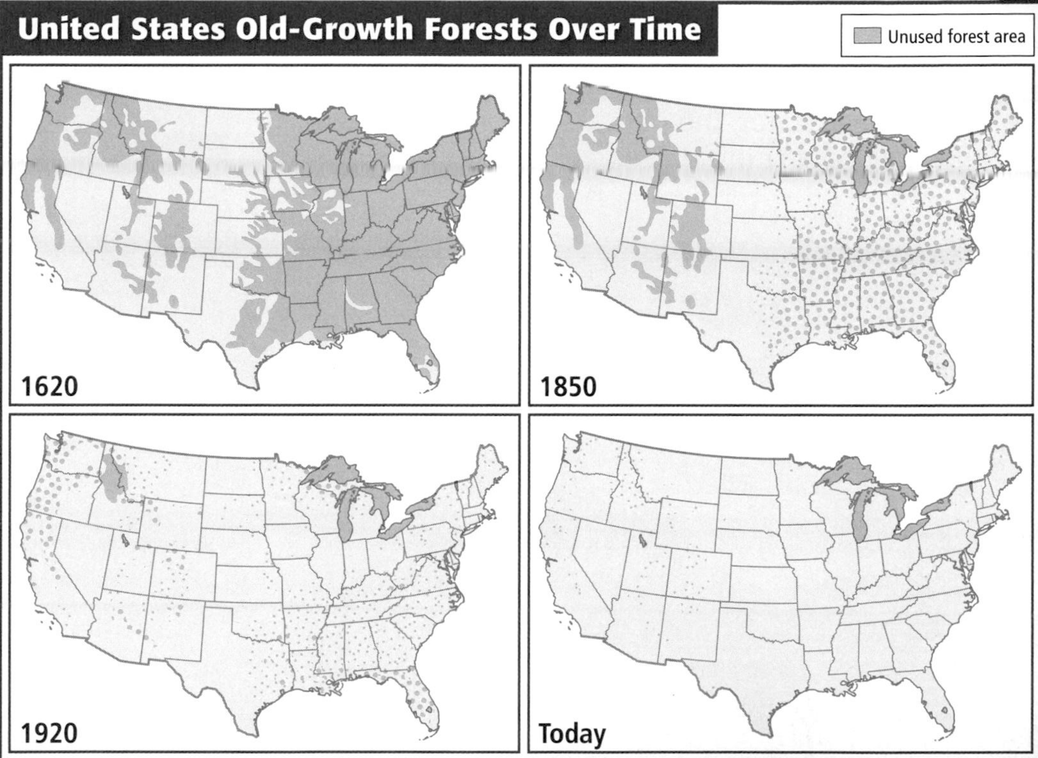

Reforestation is the process of adding forests and woodlands back into the environment. In some environments, reforestation can occur naturally. However, in many environments reforestation needs to be done by hand.

People plant trees and vegetation of many kinds in reforested areas. They try to remake what the environment would have looked like naturally. If not, the delicate balance of nature might be disturbed.

Glossary

carnivores
Animals that eat only meat. *(page 8)*

decomposers
Organisms that break down dead plants and animal waste. *(page 17)*

deforestation
The action of clearing forest areas. *(page 21)*

herbivores
Animals that eat only plants and plant products. *(page 6)*

omnivores
Animals that eat both meat and plants. *(page 10)*

reforestation
Adding forests and woodlands back into the environment. *(page 22)*

A Note to Parents

Reading books aloud and playing word games are two valuable ways parents can help their children learn to read. The easy-to-read stories in the **My First Hello Reader! With Flash Cards** series are designed to be enjoyed together. Six activity pages and 16 flash cards in each book help reinforce phonics, sight vocabulary, reading comprehension, and facility with language. Here are some ideas to develop your youngster's reading skills:

Reading with Your Child

- Read the story aloud to your child and look at the colorful illustrations together. Talk about the characters, setting, action, and descriptions. Help your child link the story to events in his or her own life.
- Read parts of the story and invite your child to fill in the missing parts. At first, pause to let your child "read" important last words in a line. Gradually, let your child supply more and more words or phrases. Then take turns reading every other line until your child can read the book independently.

Enjoying the Activity Pages

- Treat each activity as a game to be played for fun. Allow plenty of time to play.
- Read the introductory information aloud and make sure your child understands the directions.

Using the Flash Cards

- Read the words aloud with your child. Talk about the letters and sounds and meanings.
- Match the words on the flash cards with the words in the story.
- Help your child find words that begin with the same letter and sound, words that rhyme, and words with the same ending sound.
- Challenge your child to put flash cards together to make sentences from the story and create new sentences.

Above all else, make reading time together a fun time. Show your child that reading is a pleasant and meaningful activity. Be generous with your praise and know that, as your child's first and most important teacher, you are contributing immensely to his or her command of the printed word.

—Tina Thoburn, Ed.D.
Educational Consultant

ISBN 0-590-25497-9

24 23 22 21 20 19 18 17 16 01 02 03 04

Printed in the U.S.A. 24
First Scholastic printing, September 1995

I'M A FIRE FIGHTER

by Mary Packard
Illustrated by Julie Durrell

My First Hello Reader!
With Flash Cards

SCHOLASTIC INC. Cartwheel BOOKS®
New York Toronto London Auckland Sydney

Hear the bell!

Hear the siren!

DER · 10

See the truck.
See the firemen.

227

I drive the truck.

227

I see the fire.

I climb up high.
I climb up higher!

Here's the kitty.
What a day!

I grab the hose.

227

“Stop!” shouts Dad.
“I’m getting wet!”

To the Rescue!

Point to the things that fire fighters use when they put out fires.

Now point to the things that fire fighters do not use to put out fires.

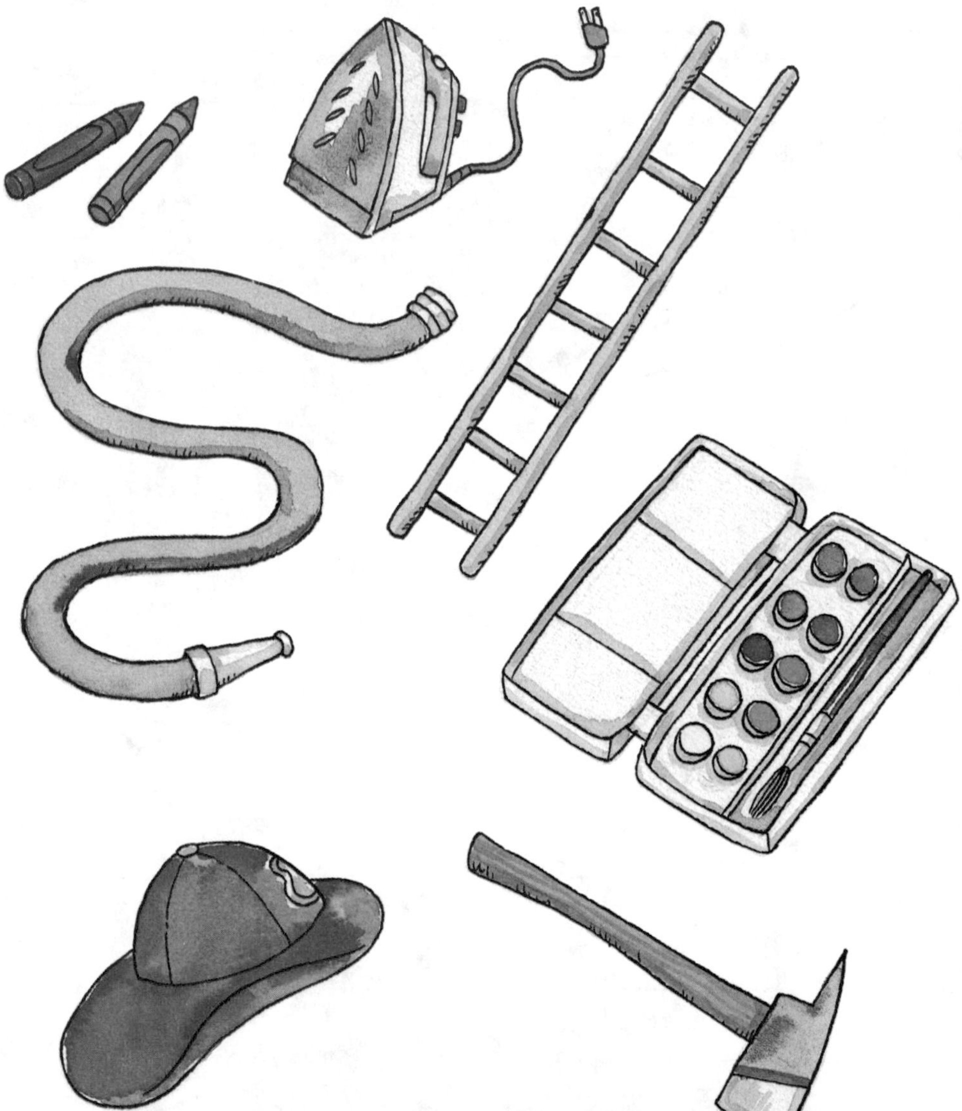

Truck Match

In each row, point to the two trucks that are the same.

These Sound Fine

Look at the pictures. Point to the pictures that begin with the same sound as:

Time to Rhyme

Rhyming words sound alike. The words **yet** and **wet** rhyme.

For each word on the left, find the word on the right that rhymes with it.

day	higher
bell	spray
fire	pretty
kitty	well

On the Move

Point to the toys that fly.

Now point to the toys that travel on the ground.

When I Grow Up

Some children think they would like to be fire fighters when they grow up. What kind of work would you like to do when you grow up?

Answers

(*To the Rescue!*)

Fire fighters use these: 

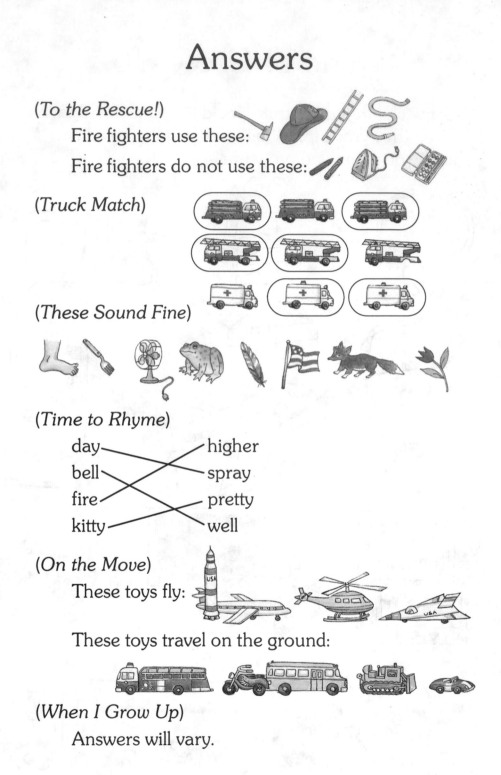

Fire fighters do not use these: 

(*Truck Match*)

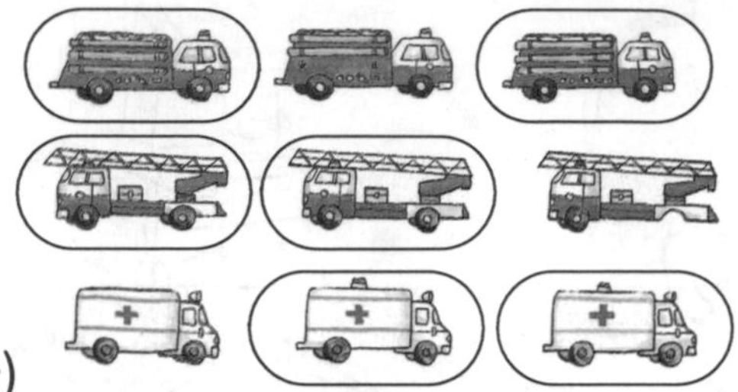

(*These Sound Fine*)

(*Time to Rhyme*)

day	higher
bell	spray
fire	pretty
kitty	well

(*On the Move*)

These toys fly: 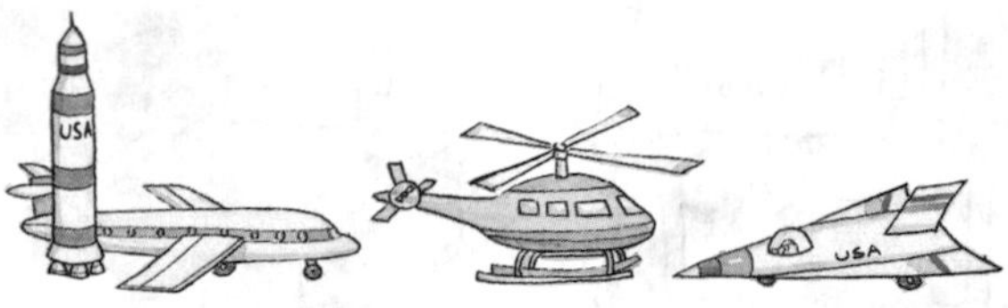

These toys travel on the ground:

(*When I Grow Up*)

Answers will vary.